More Business Wisdom Too Simple Not to Know

Richard A. Moran

A Fireside Book • Published by Simon&Schuster

FIRESIDE
Rockefeller Center
1230 Avenue of the Americas
New York, NY 10020

Designed by Bonni Leon-Berman
Manufactured in the United States of America
10   9   8   7   6   5   4   3   2   1
Library of Congress Cataloging-in-Publication Data
Moran, Richard A.
Fear no yellow stickies : more business wisdom too simple
    not to know / Richard A. Moran.
p.   cm
1. Aphorisms and apothegms.   2. Business—Quotations, maxims, etc.   I. Title.
PN6084.B87M67   1998
818' .5402—dc21   98–9750   CIP
ISBN 0-684-85219-5

To Megan, Brady, John, and Scott

And to Understanding

the Meaning of Lucky and Blessed

ACKNOWLEDGMENTS

The people I work with and observe every day are the ones who continue to provide the fodder for book material. Some are examples of the ideal way to deal with organizational issues and how to behave. Others are examples of how to make life encumbered and slow down progress. After reading the book, I'll let everyone decide for themselves on which side of the ledger they sit. I hope the people doing the real work out there never stop talking to me.

I am grateful to all my colleagues at Andersen Consulting for their support and allowances. Especially Sherry Sunderman, Susan Pearson, Bob Lauer, Steve Lamont, Steve Wilcox, Steve Elliott, Ken Dawson, Bryan Saba, John Baughn, Kathy Haden, Doug Willinger, and the rest of the Partner Group. And special thanks to Linda Meier for her patience and support.

All those who write with suggestions are a continuing source of material full of wit and wisdom. Keep the ideas coming. Special thanks to all those who contributed to this book.

Trish Todd and the staff at Simon & Schuster provided the inspiration to continue to broadcast simple but important messages.

Finally, to my family, Carol and the kids, I owe the deepest debt of gratitude for making me keep a sense of perspective.

INTRODUCTION

Behind every single aphorism in my books there is a story. Behind every "bullet" is a person or an experience. And behind every title is a larger story that, to me, truly encapsulates what's good or bad in today's organizations. The title *Fear No Yellow Stickies* is no different.

When I was once working with a large bank, one of the employees told me that his department had a yellow-stickie manager. I immediately knew exactly what he meant. His story confirmed my initial reaction.

In this particular department, the manager would respond

to every transaction with a small yellow note stuck to the edge of something. Notes would be lined up on the edge of people's desks in the morning, hung on the back of chairs and on computer screens. The most common message on the notes would be "See me ASAP" or "Who authorized this?!?" There was no need for initials at the bottom of the note, everyone knew who was sending them. And everyone dreaded them. As the employee told me, "It's to the point where we are scared to death of those x*!@%#&! yellow stickies."

There are plenty of things we should all fear in life. Yellow stickies should not be high on the list. At the bank in question, the yellow stickies had become a substitute for effective management—they were a symbol of bad management delivered efficiently.

My books are written with the intention of helping people recognize that efficiency should not replace effectiveness and that if you are doing stupid things, those around you will notice. How you are perceived and how you respond to all kinds of situations is important and will affect your career. At the very least, I'm trying to stop managers from terrorizing employees with yellow stickies. In short, I'm trying to simplify work and emphasize what is truly important.

The themes of this book are the same as those in my other books: Know how to act, take control of your own career, and maintain a balance between work and the rest of your life. All of these themes apply to both the poor soul manager who is dispensing the yellow stickies as well as to the recipients.

I hope this book will either remind or teach you about what being successful means in our increasingly complex organizations.

1. If you see your name on a yellow stickie on a conference-room wall, something very good or very bad is about to happen to you.

2. Yellow stickies with cryptic messages are not a substitute for management or communications.

3. The number of calls you receive is directly proportional to the number of calls you make.

4. Go to any meeting where food is served. If something productive also gets done in the meeting, it's a bonus.

5. Never start a meeting or a retreat with a blank sheet of paper.

6. If the right people are not in the room, don't meet.

7. When someone says they need to see you, it's really important and will only take five minutes, that person is about to resign.

8. If someone resigns, don't let the meeting take more than five minutes.

9. If you have to fire someone, it should only be a five-minute meeting. Avoid "This hurts me more than it does you."

10. If people don't understand what you're saying, don't repeat it louder and slower.

11. Unexplained absences from the office mean everyone assumes you're out interviewing.

12. Those who refuse to play office politics can be at the mercy of those who do. At least understand the game and the rules.

13. Dress conservatively, think maverick.

14. Be available. It doesn't matter that you have an open-door policy if no one can find you.

15. Point your skis down the hill at work and just go. Going sideways and backward is a much more painful way to get down the same hill.

16. Never wordsmith in a meeting. You probably have better things to do.

17. Meetings always seem to last 50 percent longer than you think they will. Plan accordingly.

18. Don't take your shoes off at work. Buy good shoes that fit instead.

19. Although it is universally despised, observe Secretaries Day.

20. Ignore National Bosses Day.

21. When "hoteling" starts at the office, consider setting up a home office.

22. Steal Hilton Hotels' motto "We can do that." Don't steal from Hilton Hotels.

23. Stop looking for more time and start looking for more ways to use the time you have.

24. Go to your high school reunion. It's a good time to reflect on whether or not you turned out as planned.

25. Damned if you do, damned if you don't are never equal. Pick the one that you believe is right.

24

26. Wave to window washers when they are suspended outside your office window.

27. If the birds are crashing into your office window, put a decal or something on it to save them from being knocked out or worse.

28. Know at least one restaurant where you can take a client or associate and not have to worry about people finding you or about the quality of the food.

29. Intolerance of other views will limit your career advancement.

30. Retirement planning can be summed up in two words: Save money.

31. Business bestseller lists are a reasonable way to determine what senior management is reading.

32. One of the most irritating things children do is smack the newspaper when you're reading it. They're right, we're wrong.

33. If you ever think, "No matter what we do, they'll come back," think again.

34. Articles in business magazines that say things like "you should be earning four times your age" make nearly everyone feel bad. Know that you're not the only one who feels those numbers can't be right.

35. Employee Activity Committees never have enough money and never make employees very active or more satisfied.

36. Employees always respond well to initiatives that will truly help the customer.

37. Making people wait for longer than five minutes is rude. Doing it chronically will label you as either rude or a poor time manager. Neither is good.

38. Learn to use the Internet well and right away.

39. Get your children to learn to use the Internet—soon.

40. When a company cuts costs, those dollars are rarely allocated for employee raises or bonuses. Set your expectations.

41. Surfing the Net can be fun, but your boss probably believes it's more like playing video games than doing your job.

42. Magazines that are not seen in the boardroom, like Spin, Rolling Stone, Details and Wired are a good source of ideas and information about what's new in music, software and videos.

43. Signing up to do something that you and everyone else knows you won't do is a test. If you don't do it and nothing happens, you win. If you don't do it and you get fired, you lose.

44. Letting your boss know you're critical of him or her, even in private, could show up on your performance review later.

45. Never give people choices you don't really want them to take.

46. If you have to fire someone, just do it. Everyone recognizes deadwood and no one likes it.

47. Faces that say "no" all the time mean the answer will almost always be "no."

48. Know where the public restrooms are on the routes you usually travel.

49. If you take your family with you on a business trip, expect to be ill prepared.

50. Dress codes should say one thing: Wear something inoffensive that would be appropriate if a client or customer showed up unannounced.

51. Wear cowboy boots with business suits only if you're from Texas, Oklahoma, or New Mexico, or if you own a herd of cattle.

52. Wait until they call your row before you stand at the door leading to the airplane.

53. Job security is an oxymoron.

54. Business casual for men means khaki pants, blue button-down collar shirt and loafers/deck shoes. Women don't need the blazer.

55. The "cycle of performance" for careers is shortening. You're only as good as your last project.

56. Some meetings divide the responsibility into such small parts that no one has any accountability.

57. In some memos, the only thing that matters is the cc's.

58. Always consider pretending to be smart even when you're clueless.

59. If a meeting can't end until someone volunteers to do something, be that volunteer.

60. Being a voice from the trenches should not give you trench mouth.

61. The fear of being dull is not a bad fear.

62. Unplanned career moves may be the most exciting. Think of those unusual offers as career dancing lessons.

63. Standing at the gate like Auntie Em and waving good-bye to Dorothy as she is about to go into Oz is bad. Be Dorothy, not Auntie Em.

64. Tell people to hold their questions until the end of a presentation only if you want very few questions or if everyone in the room reports to you.

65. We all like to sit in seats that recline, we just don't like to sit behind seats that recline. Think of that when you push the button and slam back.

66. Airplane-crash jokes are not funny.

67. Don't use obscene screen savers.

68. Early retirement opportunities should always be explored. Talk to an actuary if you don't understand it. (This may be the only time in your life you will want to talk to an actuary.)

69. When making assignments, the questions should be:

Will he/she do it?

Will he/she fit?

Will he/she know how?

70. If phone-mail systems keep cutting you off when you leave messages, your messages are too long.

71. If people aren't listening to your phone-mail messages, they are either too long or you're not saying anything.

72. Remember what it was like to show up in the classroom on test day to see a substitute teacher and learn the test was postponed? That should occasionally be duplicated at work.

73. Morale is hard to change without finding villains and punishing them.

74. Morale doesn't necessarily improve when the news for the organization is good.

75. Sharing in the misery can be a team-building exercise.

76. Lean and mean does not equate with productive and satisfied.

77. Work long hours, maintain a meaningful relationship, and raise great kids is a recipe that has never worked, and its prospects for working are dimmer all the time.

78. Without the right people in the meeting, there will be more than one meeting.

79. "Civil service mentality" is never used to describe a highly effective and efficient work group. Try to establish your working group so that it is described as the 1927 Yankees or the new way we want to be seen.

80. Know which group, function, or department are the samurai of your organization.

81. Whether affirmative-action programs stay, go, or change, making any decision that discriminates will get you fired.

82. "Back office" means you could be a target for reductions or outsourcing.

83. Rely on secondary sources only when you have to or when you must provide backup data.

84. Monday-morning staff meetings are dangerous and not as effective as ones later in the week.

85. If you schedule a Monday breakfast meeting, make sure you get home phone numbers.

86. The statement "It's just a job" is rarely true.

87. The Monday blahs are a reality. Scientists are saying it's because of what we eat and drink on weekends. Don't change what you eat or drink—just set realistic expectations for Monday.

88. Work hard on Friday so that you never feel guilty on Sunday evening for what you didn't do last week.

48

89. Bark at the moon, not at your boss.

90. If your checkbook never balances, change banks.

91. Make up songs and stories for children. They won't know the difference and you'll feel creative.

92. Supervisors who think their job is to baby-sit will be eliminated sooner or later.

93. "Narrow to one" means everyone knows what the ultimate decision will be.

94. Not being able to take your vacation when you want to or need to is bad for mental health and performance.

95. Always being below the midpoint in your salary grade means you're never going to make a lot of money.

96. If the recruitment advertising asks, "Can You Work Like This Dog?", it's either a great place with a sense of humor or a bad place to work.

97. Meetings where bad news will be delivered do not need a Johnny Carson/Ed McMahon–type setup.

98. Saying "It beats being a housewife" is not going to get you promoted.

99. Saying "You better drive" is a sign of maturity.

100. Giving customers features they are unwilling to pay for means you will either have an overly expensive product or dissatisfied customers.

101. Setting expectations is the most important part of a project.

102. No benefits, no overtime, no holiday pay means you're very dispensable.

103. When talking to someone who speaks a foreign language, don't adopt their accent.

104. In a cover-your-ass environment, the most important work is usually not done.

105. Southwest Airlines taught us all that one approach to success is to set customer expectations low but always meet those expectations.

106. Answering the question "What body in what box?" rarely produces any real change.

107. Teams at work should act and perform like basketball teams, not relay teams.

108. The phrase "line of sight" means people can see how their efforts might help achieve results. Employee morale is directly related to line of sight.

109. Teams need goals, resources, clear roles, equipment, and food.

110. Sometimes in the middle of layoffs and big changes, everyone deserves to be depressed.

111. "Sixty-fortied" is a verb not to be on the "fortied" side of.

112. Never doodle something X-rated or about other people in the room. They are likely to see it.

113. If you give your boss a ride in your car and he or she asks if you have a dog, because of the smell and the mess, always say yes.

114. Never forgetting who your friends are is a good thing to be known for.

115. Telling your boss about your sexploits will always backfire.

116. Favoritism will hurt performance and kill morale.

117. Catching up is hard to do on the job. Spend the extra hours as needed to be caught up.

118. Never leave phone-mail messages for someone at night that you'll regret in the morning.

119. Wearing Old Spice will remind everyone around you of their dad.

120. Electric razors don't work.

121. Everyone secretly likes The Three Stooges, and people usually understand jokes about them.

122. Two words to be avoided in any conversation at work are *panties* and *silly.*

123. Don't imitate Cary Grant—you can't. Don't imitate Hugh Grant either.

124. Never ask anyone why they're not married.

125. If your neighbor at work hates you, there's a fifty-fifty chance that you're a bad neighbor.

126. Always buy the property when playing Monopoly.

127. When you are put on hold, put it on the speaker and get other things done. Don't sit there and stew.

128. Watch MTV for at least fifteen minutes a week to stay semihip.

129. The Hoky Poky is what it's all about.

130. The support staff is still the backbone of almost all organizations.

131. In a meeting, talking on a cell phone is worse than carrying on a separate conversation.

132. Fall in love with a dog owner; he or she will be home at night.

133. Take ballroom dancing lessons. They will be worth it even if the only time you ever use them is at your daughter's wedding.

134. Don't send anything via E-mail that you wouldn't want to appear in your personnel file.

135. Crying at work will hurt your credibility.

64

136. E-mail programs almost always have date and time indicators. Use E-mail to your advantage by sending messages before or after regular work hours. It's a good way to show how hard you're working.

137. Spend *almost* all of your budget every year.

138. If you're really worried about something, ask yourself, What's the worst that can happen to me?

139. If you keep your car radio set on SCAN on the way home from work, you need to chill out.

140. Presentations don't have to be fancy to be effective. It's not the technology, it's the message.

141. When you describe your job and people say it's nice work if you can get it, you're lucky.

142. • Hair always looks good on the way to get it cut.

   • Pain always goes away on the way to the doctor.

   • The car always works great on the way to garage.

   • The job always seems pretty good on the way to resign.

   Be sure.

143. The most dreaded words in any presentation are: These numbers don't look right.

144. In meetings with lots of people around a table and one person on the speakerphone, talk to each other; don't yell at the phone.

145. Don't try to understand dress codes, but pay attention to them. They are more related to tradition than modesty or comfort on the job.

146. Leaving notes instructing others to clean up after themselves won't clear up the mess. Use bigger threats or hire a custodian.

147. Organizations that use military time are telling you what it's like to work there. (Airlines are the exception.)

148. Don't carry your spillproof coffee cup around all day.

149. When the early response to a job-seeking inquiry is too good, expect the job to be in telemarketing, data entry, or direct sales.

150. People can tell by watching you on the phone, without hearing you, whether you're talking to a customer or your mom.

151. If you're always saying, "In other words," you're using the wrong words.

152. Never curse during an interview, even if the interviewer does.

153. Never let anyone you work with see you naked.

154. Include your E-mail address on your business cards.

155. Every clarification of plans or strategies will breed new questions.

156. Spell-checking won't help you with the hard words or the words you use all the time.

157. When you work at home, quiet is more important than a computer.

158. Conference calls with more than four people will mean one person does all the talking.

159. Start every new job with a sense of zeal you would want others to show.

160. The three most important things to keep track of are: expenses, important phone numbers and addresses, and the last flight home.

161. Never assume that the amount you receive back will equal what you submit on your expense account.

162. Overnight packages sent for Saturday delivery are usually read on Monday morning.

163. Have your child take you into class as the exhibit for Sharing Time.

164. Yellow stickies can't hurt you. They are only an easy way to respond. Don't dread them.

165. Don't use yellow stickies as a way to threaten people.

166. Don't let people know you always use the phone-mail delete code before you listen to their messages.

167. If you eat like a child, that is, play with your food, and eat with your hands, sit in an inconspicuous spot in business meetings where food is served.

168. Downloading pornographic/offensive material from the Internet onto your work computer could get you fired and, at the least, will get you into big trouble.

169. Organizations can monitor who's doing what on the Internet through computer-activity logs. Remember, you're supposed to be working.

170. A bad credit rating sticks with you for a long time—for you and your company.

171. Organize business cards in your Rolodex by what you'll remember. Use either the name, the company, or what the person does for a living.

172. If any of the following is your work nickname, don't expect to get promoted:

- Sleepy
- Dopey
- Clueless
- The Wicked Witch
- Goofy
- Butthead
- Homer
- Gomer

173. If any of the following is your work nickname, expect to get all the special projects:
- Rambo
- Arnold
- ZoomZoom
- Steamroller
- Bulldog
- Loose Canon

174. Watch out for people with the following nicknames:
- Stinky
- Hannibal
- Loon (for lunatic)
- J.R.
- Flanders
- Archie Bunker

175. The fastest way to give yourself a raise is to work fewer hours.

176. Never assume people know why they showed up. Eighty percent of life may be showing up, but once they are there, 80 percent of success is telling them why they showed up.

177. The customer is not always right. But it's still a good place to start.

178. Using the F word with a customer service rep will never get you what you want.

179. Off-site meetings always have agendas that are way too packed. Plan to be home later than you thought.

180. Try to do the unconventional at off-site meetings. If everyone else is using overhead slides, use something else.

181. Leaders don't start anything without a vision of the outcome. Imagine Churchill going to the flip chart and turning to his staff and asking, "What do you think we should do?"

182. Know if you're a "transaction person" or a "process person." Then try to learn and use the traits of the other type.

183. The level of attention day-to-day requires is always underestimated.

184. If you don't like the answers you get, try asking different questions. Don't just repeat the same questions to your boss's boss.

84

185. Employees are almost never afraid of getting fired. They are more afraid of falling out of favor.

186. Cutting activities like holiday parties or company picnics will knock the wind out of morale, even among those who never planned to attend.

187. Artificial division of any company into executives' turfs will guarantee poor teamwork.

188. Intangible company values, like *We will be a great place to work,* are good, but neither shareholders or analysts usually care about them. That makes it harder for management to care about them.

189. Using all capital letters on E-mail is the electronic version of screaming. It's an attention grabber, but it's hard to read and hard to know what's being emphasized.

190. Cobbler's-children rules usually apply to companies. Information companies are poor at distributing information, PR firms are bad at getting their names known.

191. Low cubicle walls don't ensure low organizational walls.

192. Using E-mail is a good way to get to hard-to-reach people.

193. Hard-to-reach people will soon start having their E-mail screened and sorted.

194. When employees start counting the number of vice presidents, there are too many.

195. Change your voice mail if you're on vacation, out of town, or need to convey a specific message. It doesn't have to be every day.

196. "Let's not tell them and maybe they'll never find out," always backfires at work. It's no different from when you were a kid.

197. People stay with organizations because of their coworkers and the challenge.

198. Old computers stacked (out of their boxes) in the corners means it's either real easy or real hard to use technology in the company.

199. Warranties won't fix manufacturing problems. The problems need to be fixed in manufacturing.

200. "They" is almost always corporate staff or senior management.

201. If you're corporate staff or senior management, "they" is everybody else.

202. Parts lists are not the same as technical manuals.

203. When customer service is the last to know about new products or changes, expect the customers to be similarly uninformed.

204. Interrupt driven is a way to describe television commercials, not productive people.

205. Not fixing known problems will lead everyone to believe that there's another slew of unknown problems that aren't being fixed since no one knows about them.

206. International transposition of U.S. ways is not the same as globalization.

207. Human brakes are often applied when things get going too fast.

208. Living in the same time zone as the customer, real or imagined, is greatly appreciated.

209. Stamina is an underrated attribute for business success.

210. Labeling employees as revenue generators or nonrevenue generators will stigmatize the nons.

211. Special approvals make for special delays.

212. Individual contributor is a label to avoid if you want to be promoted. It usually means people think you lack the ability to lead a team or project.

213. Chaotic environments can make you appreciate bureaucracy.

214. Fighting over revenue or expense transfers is a very unproductive use of company time.

215. Someone *does* read employee surveys. Go ahead and attach those additional pages to express your comments.

216. Internal transfers are usually painful but worth the trouble if you want to do what you want or get away from what you don't.

217. Nicknames that could go either way depending on the organization:

- Techno Weenie
- Leona
- Prima donna
- Buttoned down

218. Being a part of a growing company does not ensure career growth.

219. Making it hard to get things done will make high turnover easier to accomplish.

220. Lack of a sense of urgency will eventually lead to lack of a job.

221. Arguing over the approach could be time well spent.

222. Expect faxes and printouts to be missing if they are not picked up within fifteen minutes.

223. Use headphones if you are playing or testing multimedia games or software.

224. Don't play multimedia games or software unless it's your job.

225. Honestly assess your value to your employer. If you think you are worth more, then you are worth more. You'll get it eventually.

226. Never look over the top of people's cubicles. It is impolite and you are intruding into their space.

227. Pay attention to your voice-mail greeting. If people begin every message by saying you sound tired or sick, change the greeting using your most upbeat FM voice.

228. Eat food with strong or bad odors anywhere but your office.

229. The rumor mill is always much faster than regular communications and usually pretty accurate.

230. Be proud of your name, whatever it is. Let people know what it is and how to pronounce it. (Special note to the artist formerly known as Prince.)

231. Airline headphones will only be comfortable for a short time. Save them for the movie.

232. Sin on the side of shaking hands too often, and introduce yourself to people who should know you.

233. Prioritize all meetings and only go to the really important ones.

234. Sit in your own assigned seat on an airplane until the door is closed.

235. Send fan mail.

236. Buy art from art school students.

237. Use the Internet to look for jobs, but only at home.

238. Free promotional computer discs received in the mail or in the Sunday newspaper are rarely free.

239. Tuck your tie into your shirt when eating on airplanes.

240. Once you quit or retire, stay away from your old workplace. They don't miss you.

241. Be known as someone who builds bridges, not fences or bombs.

242. Take medication inconspicuously. Don't line up your pills on the lunchroom table. People will assume it's Valium or lithium or worse.

243. Delegation means you don't do some of the work anymore. Don't turn delegation into duplication.

244. When your children are asked what you do, if the only response they can muster is "Go to meetings," tell them again what you do.

245. Standard operating procedures usually are not. Learn how things really get done.

246. If you yell at your coworkers constantly, they will get back at you.

247. Always know who's "got your back" at work.

248. Researchers are finding relationships between physical attractiveness and success. Hang with the good-lookers.

249. Use airplane time to reflect and set goals. It may be the closest thing to quiet time you ever get.

250. Time-outs work only with children.

251. There are hunters, skinners, and farmers at work. Golfers are not part of the equation.

252. Today 75 percent of business calls go directly into voice mail. Manage voice mail or answer the phone.

253. The line outside the door is always a sign that something real good or real bad is about to happen.

254. The more time the company spends on budget preparation, the less useful it will be. Just learn how to do it and get it in.

255. If you give callers only one minute to leave a message, get a new message system. The only one-minute message anyone will leave is "Call me back."

256. Remember that everyone laid off is someone's mom or dad or son or daughter.

257. Do a practice round before you play golf with your boss or your customer.

258. If you play golf, use good equipment—bought, begged, or borrowed. Don't get the old, faded red plaid bag off the hook in the garage.

259. Use a computer to project the presentation only if you are familiar with the technology. Don't have the audience wondering if it will work instead of what the message is.

260. Expand your casual dress wardrobe. The number of days you'll be casual will expand.

261. Clothes from Polo, The Gap, and Levi Strauss will not go out of style for casual dress.

262. Leave 90 percent of material you collect at trade shows in the hotel. Take the tchotchkes and goodies home for the kids.

263. "We're asking you to take a pay cut" is not really a question.

264. Always make a self-evaluation of performance very positive.

265. When you hear, "We'll be making hard decisions," someone will be losing their job.

266. "Honoring" bad or inappropriate behavior is not honoring.

267. "That's a good question," is rarely necessary to say. "That's a bad question" is never necessary.

268. Humor can only go so far if you're ill prepared. If there are typos throughout the presentation, stop joking about them and pointing them out after the second page.

269. Wearing a sticky paper label with VISITOR on it makes a guest feel like a tourist. If you require visitor badges, make them professional.

270. Leaving to catch a car pool is a legitimate reason to depart at a reasonable time.

271. Car-pool with people you can at least talk to.

272. Getting "written up" is the same as hearing "Wait till your father gets home."

273. Final pay decisions are often only as good as your boss's presentation skills. Take up a collection to send the boss to presentation-skills training.

274. When you are lining up all your bills every month and deciding which ones to pay, change your spending habits or change jobs.

275. There are no new complaints; they just change organizations.

276. Monthly reports are read 10 percent of the time, at most.

277. Field service people are the heroes of most organizations.

278. Never put a glazed doughnut on a mouse pad.

279. Don't leave the newspaper on the bathroom floor. Don't take it in there in the first place.

280. Plans should never be all numbers.

281. Uneven workloads will kill teamwork.

282. The word "shot" should not be used to describe displaced workers.

283. Lack of credibility will hurt you more than lack of quality.

284. When someone says, "Something good is about to happen to you," get ready to buy something.

285. Realistic planning is the easiest way to reduce stress and pressure.

286. If you're in a big company, you'll miss the "just do it" mentality; if you're in a small company, you'll miss all the support. Try to combine them.

287. Subscribe to the Deion Sanders school of career planning. We're all free agents and should go to the team that we can help and where our own needs will be met.

288. The greatest compliment is "Management does the right things."

289. Having a vision doesn't necessarily help with what we're supposed to do next week.

290. Growth almost always creates bureaucracy.

291. Buy a laptop that will fit "in the seat pocket in front of you." But never put it there; you'll lose it.

292. Learn to take two-minute vacations. Slow down to watch a child or a cloud.

293. Senders write E-mail as if they are talking. Readers see E-mail as a newspaper and expect perfect grammar and spelling. Look for the message, not the typos.

294. Phantom stock plans are never understood. No one expects the plan ever to pay out.

295. If your performance review is the same year after year, you either have a very boring job or no one is doing your review.

296. Some things won't get fixed until the Band-Aid is ripped off.

297. It's okay for a big company to have a small-company attitude. It's *not* okay for a big company to have small-company systems.

298. Sales-force incentive systems should be understood by everyone in the company, upside and downside. It's the only way nonsalespeople can deal with the trips to Hawaii.

299. Looking good on paper doesn't generate any results.

300. Schedules are not more important than quality.

301. Never feel guilty about taking a vacation.

302. Managing up is not a substitute for managing across and down.

303. Growth can hide real deficiencies until you stop growing.

304. Too much reorganizing means too much redoing.

305. When there's a light at the end of the tunnel, shorten the tunnel.

306. Great managers are good at hiring new people. Without that skill, he/she is less than good.

307. People don't want to work for a department or a division, they want to work for a company. It's all about pride.

308. Incentive plans that don't pay out create no incentives.

309. Intent is rarely the problem; it's time available and activities not completed.

310. Pace dictates the number of problems and the number of opportunities.

311. When employees start complaining about the company gym, they're probably spoiled.

312. Crisis management over a long period is not management.

313. Just because you change doesn't mean anything else has or will.

314. If you're not on the job, don't expect the supervisor to know how to do your job. He or she shouldn't need to know.

315. If you're not there, expect work to pile up.

316. Pay fluctuations based on geography are never seen as fair.

317. Dual career tracks don't move at the same speed.

318. Trainer's note:

"The perfect learner is one in a state of immediate need."
—*John Dewey*

319. Leadership school is experience, not training.

320. A bad phone system can shut down the entire plant.

321. When you ask someone how he or she gets so much done, the answer usually includes: "I don't watch TV."

322. Flush is what we do in the bathroom, not the way we add more details as in, We are going to flesh out the proposal.

323. Work elimination is still way behind people elimination, so set your expectations.

324. Some people work hard, some people make a lot of money.

325. Categorizing lots of problems into simple buckets makes it seem like there are not as many.

326. Go to bat to get your company to contribute to a worthy not-for-profit organization. Even if it seems futile, you'll feel better.

327. Rock bottom is always deeper than you think.

328. Treating people like numbers will prevent the company from meeting its numbers.

329. Policies can either set standards or provide guidelines. Don't have all one or the other.

330. If you're dating a coworker, tell your boss at the right time.

331. When all else has failed, return to basics.

332. Pay your parking tickets, even if you get them in rental cars in far away from home cities. They will catch up to you.

333. Learn how not to lose things, to avoid insanity. Learn especially how not to lose checkbooks and credit cards.

334. The best examples of process efficiency are usually in take-out delis. Pay attention at lunch.

335. When you hear anything close to "We're not going to get any smarter about this," just make the decision.

336. The answer to any business issue is never "All we are is dust in the wind."

337. Employee relations people are always depressed.

338. At least 50 percent of any project is putting together the to-do list or plan.

339. If you have to ask if there's a conflict of interest, there probably is.

340. Two words to carefully listen for in a performance review are "but" and "however."

341. There is a big difference between working as a club and working as a team. Most organizations confuse the two.

342. Interim is not a good spot to be in.

343. Assignment of blame through computer codes and forms will lead to games and no one owning the problem.

344. Take all the NO FEAR decals off your car before you give your boss his or her first ride.

345. If cab drivers want to talk, they'll let you know.

346. Change your dream from a Porsche to a plush minivan as soon as you have children. It's not whether, it's when.

347. A stint in the military can still be the right career choice. Don't miss it.

348. Think long-range planning for events that require wearing a bathing suit.

349. With people you know but haven't seen for a while, take the risk and say hello. They remember too.

350. Never admit you went South of the Border.

351. Act as if you are someday going to run for public office.

352. If it's too late to run for office, act that way anyway.

353. Beware of friendly people at East Coast (U.S.) airports. It's the mean people who are there to help you.

354. Death certificates should never be required if an employee asks for a bereavement day.

355. Hand-held computers are best for calendars, phone numbers, and to-do lists. Keep taking meeting notes in the spiral notebook.

356. People who work in high technology are always late. That's no excuse.

357. Wear nose rings only if you work for MTV, a messenger service, or yourself.

358. Check phone mail, E-mail and U.S. mail in that order. Learn all delete functions quickly.

359. There are no job hoppers, only opportunists.

360. There is not necessarily a relationship between how long someone is employed and their qualifications.

361. Cash bonus checks as soon as you receive them.

362. Occasionally pay the toll for the driver behind you.

363. Don't send your blue jeans to the dry cleaners. They will come back with a crease as if they'd been ironed and hurt the perceptions others have of you.

364. There is a rhythm to work and to each job. Get in the rhythm; it makes the job easier.

365. When people give you the finger on the highway, don't let it hurt your feelings.

366. When a customer starts preaching about partnering, get ready for a request for a price reduction.

367. Be careful when someone in the purchasing department starts saying "It's a two-way street."

368. The race at work is not always won by the swift, and there is more to life than increasing its speed.

369. Don't say "Pardon my French." Either curse and mean it or don't curse at all.

370. Four dreaded words in any situation are: See attendant for key.

371. God invented car phones for two reasons. The first is so that you can call to say you're running late. The second is for calling the pizza delivery service from the road so that you can be met at your door.

372. Unless you're a surgeon or an airline pilot, always remember that as much as you like or dislike your job, it's still just a job.

EPILOGUE

Not too long ago I received a piece of fan mail that caught my attention more than others. All authors love mail, and in this particular note, the fan claimed I had changed his life. As a result of reading my books he was now happy and at peace with his work and life. I wrote back with a list of books that he might really want to read for life-changing perspectives. I have no grand notions that I am changing anyone's life, but I do believe these simple messages do make a difference. Let me hear from you with your own "bullets" for success. I am grateful to all those who contributed to this book. Write to me at the following address:

Richard A. Moran
P.O. Box 29134
San Francisco, CA 94129-0134

CONTRIBUTORS

The following individuals and groups generated ideas, made suggestions, and sent in aphorisms that were considered or used:

Chris Bauer

Kenrick L. Brathwaite

Paula Rice Carlson

Jon Carroll

Thomas S. Case

Bert Flynn

Lura Flynn

Douglas Gillanders

Linda Hergenhahn

Karl C. Kriegsmann

Barbara Landy

Jack Moran and the ASCO gang

Norman Muchnick

Barbara R. Munro

Julie A. Oke

Michael J. Pierce

Rob Welbourn

Debra M. Zaslav

ABOUT THE AUTHOR

Richard A. Moran is a Partner with Andersen Consulting LLP in Change Management. He has worked in all types of organizations worldwide. Moran helps organizations implement their strategies by keeping management focused and by getting lots of help from employees. He is the coauthor of the 1993 landmark study *Postcards from Employees,* which captures the perceptions of more than 50,000 employees regarding their organizations and managements as well as customer service and other work-related areas. He has been featured on CNN, National Public Radio, UPI, and other media on workplace and employee issues. Moran lives with his family in San Francisco.